TRUE CONNECTION

Mastering Trust and Emotional Intimacy

Ged Clark

Title: *True Connection: Mastering Trust and Emotional Intimacy*
Author: Ged Clark
ISBN: 9798345483176

TABLE OF CONTENTS

Introduction

The Power of True Connection

In an increasingly fast-paced world filled with surface-level interactions, finding true connection can feel elusive. We scroll through feeds, tap out quick replies, and manage a network of contacts, yet often find ourselves yearning for something deeper something more enduring and meaningful. *True Connection: Mastering Trust and Emotional Intimacy* is about this very pursuit: how we build relationships that go beyond the superficial, relationships that not only fulfill us but also challenge us to grow, to open up, and to live more authentically.

Relationships are central to our existence, woven into the fabric of our everyday lives. Yet many of us struggle with understanding the dynamics that make relationships strong, resilient, and deeply fulfilling. We all want to feel seen, valued, and understood, but these qualities don't always come naturally. Instead, they're cultivated through trust, vulnerability, and clear, honest communication. This book invites you to explore each of these foundational elements, helping you to strengthen the bonds you hold dear and create new, authentic connections that add joy and depth to your life.

Why We Struggle to Connect

For many people, building trust and intimacy can be challenging. We may carry past wounds from relationships where trust was broken, or we may have learned to guard ourselves as a way of self-preservation. Vulnerability can feel risky and uncomfortable; it exposes us, requiring us to let go of control and face the possibility of rejection. But the truth is that without vulnerability, there can be no intimacy. Without trust, relationships lack the foundation needed to withstand life's inevitable challenges.

Our society often emphasizes independence and self-sufficiency, values that can, ironically, keep us isolated. In our quest to protect ourselves, we sometimes miss out on the beauty of truly sharing life with others our triumphs, our fears, and even our everyday moments. When we choose to show up authentically, however, we offer others the space to do the same, creating a dynamic of mutual trust and respect. This book is designed to guide you on this path of openness and connection, teaching you how to embrace the courage it takes to build lasting bonds.

Building a Foundation of Trust

Trust is the cornerstone of any meaningful relationship. Without it, we operate in a space of doubt, suspicion, and self-protection. Trust creates a safe environment for us to express our needs, our fears, and our hopes. It allows us to know that someone will be there, not just when it's convenient, but also when it's hard. This guide will show you how to build and sustain trust, even when obstacles arise, and how to rebuild it when it's been compromised. Real-life examples and practical exercises are provided throughout to help you see how trust works in the real world and how it deepens over time.

Embracing Vulnerability

The idea of vulnerability can be unsettling, conjuring images of rejection, judgment, or exposure. Yet, vulnerability is the gateway to genuine connection. It requires us to lower our defenses and to be honest about who we are, even when it's uncomfortable. Vulnerability asks us to share our emotions and to trust that those we care about will respond with empathy and understanding. By facing this challenge, we allow intimacy to flourish, building connections that are rich in understanding and mutual support.

In the chapters to come, we'll explore why vulnerability is essential and how to move past the fears that keep us guarded. You'll discover techniques to help you embrace openness gradually, fostering a sense of security within yourself and in your relationships. Vulnerability, as you'll learn, is not a sign of weakness but a profound act of courage and strength.

The Art of Open Communication

Communication is more than simply speaking and listening; it is a dance of words, body language, and timing. How we communicate affects every aspect of our relationships, shaping the ways we connect, understand, and support each other. Misunderstandings and unmet expectations often arise not from a lack of care but from a lack of clarity. In this book, we'll dive into techniques for expressing needs and listening mindfully, turning everyday conversations into opportunities for connection.

We'll cover how to approach difficult conversations, handle conflicts constructively, and ensure that both parties feel heard and valued. The goal is not to avoid disagreements but to navigate them in a way that strengthens the relationship, creating a shared language that is honest, compassionate, and constructive.

The Journey to Lasting Connections

True Connection is more than a book; it's an invitation to transform the way you approach relationships. With each chapter, you'll discover practical tools and insights that will help you cultivate deeper connections with family, friends, romantic partners, and even within yourself. You'll learn how to overcome obstacles to intimacy, such as fear, misunderstandings, and past hurts, empowering you to create relationships that are resilient and fulfilling.

This journey is not a quick fix but a lifelong practice of showing up, reaching out, and being present for those who matter most. As you work through the principles of trust, vulnerability, and open communication, you'll find yourself building a network of relationships rooted in authenticity, respect, and mutual support. These connections will not only enrich your life but also provide a foundation of stability and joy, whatever challenges you may face.

So, let's embark on this journey together. May these pages inspire you to take meaningful steps toward true connection, opening the door to relationships that bring genuine happiness, growth, and satisfaction. Whether you are looking to deepen an existing relationship or start fresh, you're about to begin a path of discovery that leads to richer, more rewarding connections. Here's to mastering trust, embracing vulnerability, and building a life full of authentic, lasting bonds.

Chapter 1:

The Foundation of Trust

Trust is the bedrock of every meaningful relationship. It is the sense of safety we feel in the presence of another, knowing we can rely on them to be honest, consistent, and supportive. Without trust, relationships struggle to flourish; with it, they grow, deepen, and weather storms. Trust creates a stable environment, where both individuals can be vulnerable, honest, and open, paving the way for emotional intimacy and lasting connection.

In any relationship, trust emerges from consistency, transparency, and reliability. To trust someone means believing that they will show up as they say they will, be truthful about their actions and feelings, and remain steady, especially in times of conflict or uncertainty. When trust is established, a space for honest, heartfelt exchanges becomes possible, allowing both parties to express themselves freely, without fear of judgment or betrayal.

To fully understand the role of trust, let's look at how it forms, grows, and sometimes breaks down in relationships. At its core, trust-building involves a blend of small, everyday actions and conscious, repeated efforts. The ways we speak, listen, and respond to one another shape our connections. Consistency, for instance, builds trust because it reassures us of a person's reliability. When someone is consistent, they demonstrate that they can be counted on, and this pattern fosters confidence. Similarly, transparency invites us to trust by allowing us to see the truth of a person's intentions and feelings. When someone is honest even in uncomfortable situations we learn to rely on their word. Finally, reliability, which combines both consistency and transparency, is crucial because it assures us that a person's words align with their actions. When people say what they mean and do what they say, we experience the stability that supports trust.

However, trust is fragile. Even a single act of dishonesty or inconsistency can shake the foundation of a relationship. For instance, if a friend cancels plans repeatedly or hides something significant, it can erode our sense of security with them. Research shows that our brains respond to breaches in trust as a form of emotional pain, not unlike physical pain, because the feeling of betrayal activates similar neurological pathways. This reaction makes sense; when trust is broken, the security of the relationship is threatened, and rebuilding that trust takes conscious, consistent effort over time.

Rebuilding trust after it has been damaged is a delicate process. It requires both parties to confront the reasons behind the breach and address any underlying issues. For the person who has broken the trust, actions speak louder than words. Apologies are important, but more essential is a change in behavior that restores reliability. This may include small, everyday acts of showing up on time, being honest even when it's uncomfortable, and following through on commitments. It's also helpful to set boundaries that give both individuals the space to heal. In relationships where trust has been severely damaged, gradual steps can rebuild a foundation, allowing both parties to redefine their expectations and commitments.

Re-establishing trust also means working on oneself. We each bring to our relationships a collection of past experiences and perceptions that influence how we trust others. If someone has experienced betrayal or loss in the past, they may find it difficult to trust easily. In these cases, recognizing and addressing these personal influences can be beneficial. Sometimes, speaking with a counselor or coach can help individuals explore their own "trust blueprint," allowing them to identify patterns, manage insecurities, and ultimately create healthier, more resilient connections.

To help strengthen trust in our own lives, here are a few exercises and tips:

1. **Practice Active Listening**: When someone speaks, make it a habit to listen without interrupting or formulating a

response in your mind. Show that you value their words by asking follow-up questions and making an effort to understand their perspective fully.

2. **Keep Small Promises**: Trust is built in the small moments as much as in the big ones. Make it a priority to keep promises, even minor ones, like showing up on time or following through on a planned activity. These small acts reinforce reliability.

3. **Be Transparent About Feelings**: If you're uncomfortable with a situation, communicate it respectfully. Share your feelings openly, even if it feels vulnerable. Doing so will encourage others to do the same and create a culture of honesty within the relationship.

4. **Apologize and Take Accountability**: Mistakes happen, and acknowledging them honestly goes a long way. A genuine apology, coupled with actions to make amends, signals that you value the relationship and are willing to correct your mistakes.

5. **Stay Present and Engaged**: When spending time with someone, be fully present. Put away distractions and make an effort to engage. Showing genuine interest communicates that you value the person and strengthens your connection.

6. **Reaffirm Commitments**: Periodically check in on important relationships, affirming your commitment to trust and transparency. This simple act can help both parties feel reassured and valued, which deepens the bond.

Building trust is an ongoing process; it requires patience, commitment, and openness. Yet, as we take steps toward showing up authentically, the rewards in our relationships are profound. Trust becomes the safety net, a steady presence that allows each person to feel secure, connected, and valued. When we invest in trust, we create a foundation that can sustain any relationship, allowing it to grow into something rich and fulfilling over time.

In addition to the practical exercises mentioned, it's also crucial to recognize that trust isn't static; it evolves with time and experience. As we grow and our relationships deepen, trust becomes an ongoing, dynamic exchange. Each interaction whether big or small presents an opportunity to reinforce or challenge the trust we share with others. In this way, trust becomes an active commitment rather than a fixed quality, encouraging us to continually nurture the bonds that matter most.

One key aspect of fostering trust is **mutual respect**. Respect forms the foundation for all interactions in a relationship and serves as a guiding principle during disagreements or misunderstandings. Trust isn't about always agreeing; rather, it's about respecting each other's perspectives, even when they differ. When both parties feel respected, they're more willing to be vulnerable and honest, knowing that their thoughts and feelings are valued.

Setting healthy boundaries also plays a central role in trust-building. Boundaries are not barriers; they're safeguards that define personal needs and ensure that both individuals feel respected and comfortable. By expressing our boundaries openly, we invite others to understand us more fully, which leads to a sense of mutual trust and respect. Boundaries also help prevent misunderstandings and resentment, as both individuals are aware of each other's limits and expectations.

In many cases, trust involves **managing expectations**. It's common for unspoken assumptions to lead to disappointment or frustration when our needs aren't met. However, clear communication about expectations whether they pertain to time, emotional support, or shared responsibilities can help prevent misunderstandings and strengthen the foundation of the relationship. When we communicate our needs openly, we not only build trust but also create an environment where both individuals can thrive.

Trust also requires us to show **empathy** in moments of vulnerability. When someone shares something personal, it's an invitation for us to respond with understanding and care. Empathy, in turn, nurtures a sense of closeness that deepens trust. By putting ourselves in another person's shoes and genuinely seeking to understand their perspective, we demonstrate that we're reliable and emotionally available, even during difficult times. This empathy fosters a connection that transcends surface-level interactions, allowing both individuals to feel seen, heard, and valued.

Finally, trust involves accepting that **imperfections are part of every relationship**. No one is perfect, and no relationship will be without its struggles. Accepting these imperfections allows us to view conflicts as opportunities for growth rather than signs of failure. When trust is present, individuals feel secure enough to address issues openly, fostering a resilient relationship that can adapt and evolve over time.

Through these practices consistency, transparency, respect, empathy, boundaries, and managing expectations we lay the groundwork for trust that is both deep and enduring. Trust not only enhances our relationships but also enriches our personal well-being, giving us the confidence to be our authentic selves and share in genuine connection.

Chapter 2:

Embracing Vulnerability for Deeper Connection

Vulnerability can feel like stepping out onto a ledge with nothing to hold on to, yet it is the very thing that makes relationships meaningful. Vulnerability invites us to open up, share our genuine selves, and let others in, exposing both our strengths and our fears. Although vulnerability might feel risky, it is one of the most powerful ways to foster emotional intimacy. Through vulnerability, we let others see who we truly are, creating a pathway to empathy, understanding, and ultimately, trust.

In relationships, vulnerability acts as the bridge between people, breaking down barriers that otherwise keep us from connecting authentically. When we allow ourselves to be vulnerable, we give others the chance to see us beyond our social facades or the defenses we've built to protect ourselves. This openness is the foundation of trust, as it shows that we are willing to take emotional risks, demonstrating that we care about a relationship enough to be seen in our entirety. Vulnerability, then, becomes the medium through which we communicate trust, value, and respect for another person.

Yet, for many, being vulnerable doesn't come naturally. It's a challenge we often avoid, fearing that exposure will lead to rejection, judgment, or even betrayal. Society has conditioned many of us to equate vulnerability with weakness, associating emotional exposure with risk rather than strength. But real vulnerability isn't about exposing our innermost feelings all the time or in every context. It's about learning to be honest and open in a balanced, intentional way that brings people closer rather than pushing them away.

One reason vulnerability can feel daunting is that it opens the door to the unknown. When we share our insecurities or our hopes with someone, we give them a glimpse into our inner world. The outcome of this openness isn't guaranteed, which can trigger feelings of anxiety or self-doubt. However, the beauty of vulnerability lies in its ability to encourage growth. With each step toward openness, we strengthen our ability to connect on a deeper level, building a solid foundation where both people feel safe to express their true selves.

To understand vulnerability's transformative potential, consider a real-life example: a couple navigating a period of tension after years of marriage. Both partners may feel frustrated, misunderstood, or even disconnected. Yet, by daring to be vulnerable, they can break through the cycle of resentment and miscommunication. Instead of defensively stating complaints, each person can take a different approach, sharing what truly underlies their frustrations. Perhaps one partner feels unappreciated, while the other feels overwhelmed by responsibilities. By speaking honestly about their emotions, they allow each other to connect on a deeper level, empathizing rather than reacting. Vulnerability reframes the conversation, helping them see each other's perspectives and paving the way for healing and understanding.

In friendships, vulnerability also deepens connection. Think about two friends who have drifted apart over time. Rather than allowing the distance to continue growing, one of them might reach out to share how much the friendship means to them and how they miss spending time together. This openness requires courage, as it risks the possibility of unreciprocated feelings. However, this simple act of sharing invites the other friend to respond with their own feelings, often leading to reconnection and a strengthened bond. By taking the first step toward vulnerability, we allow our relationships to be refreshed, bringing closeness and mutual appreciation back into the dynamic.

For those looking to practice vulnerability, role-playing exercises can be a helpful start. These activities can be done alone or with a partner, offering a safe way to explore the dynamics of vulnerability without the immediate pressure of "real" emotional risks. In one exercise, each person can take turns sharing something meaningful; a personal story, a hope, a fear, or a memory that reveals something about their inner world. By setting a supportive atmosphere where both parties commit to listening without judgment, this activity fosters a space of mutual respect and openness. Through these exercises, people can practice finding the words to express themselves, learning how to open up gradually while feeling safe.

Another powerful exercise for embracing vulnerability is writing a letter to oneself or to a loved one. In this letter, express any emotions or experiences that might feel too difficult to say out loud. This process allows you to explore your feelings without fear of judgment, gaining clarity and insight. Writing can help us identify the core of our emotions, often revealing the deeper needs behind our initial reactions. If comfortable, consider sharing the letter with the person involved, using it as a starting point for a conversation. Such expressions can be deeply affirming, as they often lead to greater understanding and compassion from both sides.

One of the key aspects of practicing vulnerability is learning to recognize and honor our boundaries. Being vulnerable doesn't mean sharing every aspect of our lives or compromising our sense of safety. Healthy vulnerability involves respecting both our own boundaries and those of others. It's about sharing with intention, being open in ways that feel appropriate and balanced for each situation. For instance, in the early stages of a relationship, vulnerability might look like sharing hopes and values. As trust grows, it may deepen into sharing fears, insecurities, or past experiences. Respecting this pace helps ensure that vulnerability strengthens rather than strains the relationship.

Through each experience of vulnerability, we gradually develop the courage to be more open in our relationships. This journey is one of small, steady steps, building trust and connection with each moment of authenticity. As we continue to embrace vulnerability, we also inspire others to do the same, creating a positive cycle of openness and understanding in our relationships. Vulnerability, then, becomes more than a risk it becomes a way of honoring ourselves and those we care about, giving everyone involved the gift of authentic, meaningful connection.

When we fully embrace vulnerability, we allow our relationships to move beyond surface-level exchanges and into spaces where true connection can flourish. This willingness to show our authentic selves encourages others to open up as well, creating a foundation for mutual growth, empathy, and respect. The bonds formed through shared vulnerability are often more resilient, as they are based on genuine understanding rather than assumptions or pretenses.

In romantic relationships, vulnerability invites each partner to explore and understand each other's inner worlds. It allows couples to communicate more effectively by moving beyond defensive reactions or assumptions. For example, instead of saying, "You never listen to me," one partner might express, "I feel unheard when I share things that matter to me, and that hurts." This reframing takes courage but can completely transform the dynamic by highlighting underlying emotions rather than placing blame. The vulnerability of expressing hurt or disappointment directly can be the key to breaking negative patterns, inviting each partner to respond with empathy instead of defensiveness. Through this process, couples learn to face issues as a team rather than as individuals in conflict, creating a relationship dynamic based on partnership rather than opposition.

The impact of vulnerability in family relationships is similarly profound. In parent-child relationships, for instance, parents who are vulnerable with their children create a model of openness that fosters trust. By sharing their own struggles, hopes, or even mistakes in an age-appropriate way, parents show children that it's okay to experience and express a full range of emotions. This openness often makes children feel more comfortable sharing their own feelings, reinforcing a secure attachment based on emotional transparency. As children grow, they carry this model of vulnerability with them, applying it to other relationships and contributing to a generational cycle of openness and empathy.

In friendships, vulnerability strengthens the foundation of trust by allowing friends to understand each other on a deeper level. When friends share personal fears, goals, or setbacks, it builds solidarity and provides opportunities for mutual support. Imagine a friend confiding about a major life transition, such as starting a new job, moving to a new city, or navigating a breakup. By listening, affirming, and even sharing a similar experience, the other friend has the chance to foster a connection rooted in empathy and support. These acts of vulnerability can transform friendships from casual acquaintances to true sources of strength, making each person feel seen and valued.

Professional relationships, while often more formal, also benefit from appropriate expressions of vulnerability. In work environments, showing vulnerability can improve teamwork and collaboration, as it encourages an atmosphere of psychological safety. When a leader admits to not having all the answers or shares a lesson learned from a past mistake, it models humility and authenticity for the team. Colleagues, in turn, may feel more comfortable sharing ideas, asking questions, or admitting when they need help, leading to a work culture that values growth over perfection. Vulnerability in professional settings doesn't mean oversharing but rather demonstrating honesty in a way that promotes trust and accountability among team members.

The journey to embracing vulnerability often requires overcoming deeply rooted fears and learning to trust both oneself and others. Many of us have built protective walls due to past hurts or disappointments, and lowering those defenses can feel intimidating. But as we practice small acts of vulnerability, we become more comfortable with emotional exposure, recognizing that it isn't about weakness but about embracing life fully. Vulnerability allows us to experience richer relationships, greater self-acceptance, and a sense of empowerment that comes from showing up authentically.

Ultimately, embracing vulnerability isn't about achieving perfect relationships. It's about building real, resilient connections that support us through life's ups and downs. Vulnerability brings a depth to relationships that helps them withstand inevitable conflicts or challenges. Through vulnerability, we give our loved ones a chance to truly know us, and in turn, we experience the profound gift of being truly known. By opening ourselves up to others, we also open ourselves to the joys of shared experience, mutual understanding, and the enduring bond that vulnerability brings to all relationships.

In the end, vulnerability is the heartbeat of connection. It allows us to break free from isolation and invites others into our lives in meaningful ways. Embracing vulnerability doesn't remove the risks of being hurt or misunderstood, but it gives us the tools to move through those moments with courage and resilience. Vulnerability invites growth, trust, and emotional intimacy that transforms relationships and enriches our lives, offering a lasting foundation for deeper, more fulfilling connections.

Chapter 3:

The Art of Communication for Lasting Connection

Communication is the lifeline of any meaningful relationship. While words are important, true communication goes beyond spoken language; it encompasses body language, tone, timing, and the intention behind each exchange. Each of these elements can either bridge or widen the gap between two people. When we learn to communicate mindfully, we open doors to understanding, empathy, and trust strengthening the bonds that matter most to us.

One of the most powerful tools in effective communication is **mindful listening**. Listening with full presence is a rare skill, but it makes a world of difference in any relationship. Often, we listen with the intent to respond, forming our replies in our heads while the other person is still speaking. This kind of listening can lead to misunderstandings and frustrations. Instead, mindful listening involves quieting our internal dialogue and focusing on what the other person is truly saying. This means observing not just the words they use, but also their tone, pace, and body language. This level of engagement signals respect and interest, showing the speaker that we value their thoughts and feelings.

Mindful listening also requires patience. Silence, often uncomfortable in conversation, is necessary to give others the time and space to express themselves fully. If we rush to fill every silence, we may miss important cues about the other person's emotions or intentions. By letting pauses occur naturally, we invite more meaningful responses and create a space where both people feel safe to explore their thoughts.

Another valuable skill in effective communication is the ability to ask open-ended questions. Instead of questions that lead to simple "yes" or "no" answers, open-ended questions invite reflection and deeper conversation. These questions begin with "how," "what," or "why," and they encourage the other person to elaborate. For example, instead of asking, "Did you have a good day?" which limits the response, you might ask, "What was something interesting that happened today?" This question invites the person to share more, often leading to conversations that reveal more about their inner world and experiences.

Alongside listening and asking questions, expressing needs openly is an essential part of building trust in relationships. Often, we expect others to understand our needs without us having to say them aloud, assuming they should just "know." This unspoken expectation can lead to resentment and disappointment when those needs aren't met. By learning to articulate our needs directly, we take ownership of our desires and create an atmosphere where our loved ones can support us more effectively. For instance, instead of hinting at feeling overwhelmed, try saying, "I could really use some support with this project. Could we spend some time working on it together?" This kind of open communication invites collaboration and helps both people feel understood and valued.

However, even with the best intentions, misunderstandings can still arise. One of the most common communication pitfalls is assuming that the other person interprets our words and actions the same way we do. Each person comes into a conversation with their own set of experiences, beliefs, and emotional triggers, which shape how they perceive what is being said. Recognizing this difference is key to avoiding misunderstandings. When conflict arises, instead of assuming the other person understands our point of view, it's helpful to clarify our thoughts and ask questions to ensure that we understand theirs.

For instance, consider a situation where a couple has a disagreement over household responsibilities. One person might interpret a request for help as criticism, while the other sees it as a simple request. In this case, clarifying each person's perspective can help prevent escalation. One partner might say, "When I asked for help with the dishes, I didn't mean to imply you aren't doing enough, I just felt overwhelmed." This clarification allows the other person to see the request for what it is and not as a criticism. Taking the time to clarify intentions can de-escalate misunderstandings and create a sense of safety, allowing each person to communicate more openly.

Another crucial aspect of navigating disagreements is shifting our mindset from **winning an argument to seeking understanding**. In moments of conflict, it's easy to fall into the habit of defending our perspective or proving our point. However, this approach can turn discussions into battles, where one person "wins" at the cost of the other's feelings or perspective. Instead, a focus on understanding each other's viewpoint creates a collaborative environment where both people feel heard and valued.

One helpful technique is to repeat back what the other person has said, confirming that we understand their point before sharing our own. For example, saying, "I hear that you're feeling unappreciated because of how busy I've been with work. I'm sorry for that. I'd like to understand how I can show you more appreciation," shows the other person that their feelings are recognized. This acknowledgment doesn't require agreement but demonstrates that you're listening and prioritizing their emotions. Once both parties feel heard, they're usually more open to finding a compromise or solution.

In addition to listening, asking questions, and expressing needs, building a **shared language** within relationships is a valuable strategy. Over time, couples, friends, and family members often develop a unique language that includes terms, phrases, or gestures that hold special meaning. This language strengthens bonds and provides a shorthand for expressing thoughts or emotions, often without needing lengthy explanations. For example, a simple word or phrase could serve as a reminder of shared goals or commitments, helping both parties reconnect to their shared values when conflicts arise. This language becomes a shared toolkit that supports understanding and provides comfort during difficult moments.

Communication is also about timing. Choosing the right moment to address important topics can make a significant difference in the outcome of a conversation. Bringing up sensitive issues when the other person is tired, stressed, or distracted can lead to a defensive reaction or a superficial discussion. Instead, timing conversations when both parties are present and open allows for more meaningful exchanges. Being mindful of timing shows respect for the other person's state of mind and ensures that important topics receive the attention they deserve.

Finally, practicing **forgiveness** in communication is essential. Missteps are inevitable, and everyone occasionally says or does something they regret. When this happens, offering forgiveness and accepting apologies is key to moving forward. This doesn't mean ignoring hurt feelings but rather allowing room for repair and growth. Holding grudges or continually bringing up past mistakes can create a negative cycle that undermines trust. By forgiving and letting go of past misunderstandings, we create a culture of resilience in our relationships.

Communication is an ongoing practice, a balance of speaking, listening, and observing. When we commit to communicating authentically and respectfully, we build relationships that can withstand challenges and bring us closer to the people we care about. In the end, communication isn't just about exchanging information it's about creating connections, fostering trust, and cultivating a deeper sense of intimacy that enriches every aspect of our lives.

Through the ongoing practice of authentic communication, we create a foundation that allows relationships to thrive. As we engage in mindful listening, ask open-ended questions, and express our needs openly, we foster an environment where trust can flourish. This environment encourages vulnerability, where both parties feel safe to share their thoughts and emotions without fear of judgment or ridicule.

However, to truly harness the power of communication, we must also be willing to confront our own barriers. Fear, anxiety, and past experiences can hinder our ability to communicate effectively. For some, the fear of rejection or conflict may lead to avoidance, while others may struggle with expressing emotions due to cultural or familial conditioning. Recognizing these barriers is the first step toward overcoming them. We can begin by reflecting on our communication habits and identifying areas where we feel comfortable and where we struggle.

One helpful exercise is to keep a communication journal. This journal can serve as a space to reflect on daily interactions, noting both successes and challenges. For example, after a conversation that felt particularly meaningful, take a moment to write down what made it successful. What questions did you ask? How did you express your needs? Conversely, after a conflict, jot down what went wrong. Did you interrupt? Were you defensive?

This practice of reflection allows us to see patterns in our communication and identify specific areas for growth.

Another important aspect of effective communication is learning to manage our emotions. When discussions become heated, our emotional responses can cloud our judgment and prevent us from communicating effectively. Techniques such as deep breathing, pausing before responding, or even taking a break can help us regain our composure and approach conversations with a clearer mind. Practicing emotional regulation enables us to engage in discussions without being overwhelmed by our feelings, allowing for more constructive and open exchanges.

Furthermore, understanding the **role of empathy** in communication cannot be overstated. Empathy is the ability to put ourselves in another person's shoes, to feel what they feel, and to respond with compassion. When we approach conversations with empathy, we create a connection that transcends mere words. For instance, when a friend expresses frustration about a challenging situation, instead of offering quick solutions or dismissing their feelings, we can say, "It sounds like you're feeling really overwhelmed right now. I'm here for you." This empathetic response validates their emotions and encourages a deeper dialogue.

Additionally, it's essential to recognize that communication is not a one-way street; it requires active participation from both parties. Effective communication relies on a balance of speaking and listening. When both individuals engage equally, they create a dynamic that fosters understanding and connection. This reciprocal communication can be achieved by establishing ground rules for discussions, such as taking turns to speak and ensuring that both parties have an opportunity to share their thoughts without interruption.

As we navigate the complexities of relationships, it is crucial to remember that effective communication is not about perfection but about progress. Each conversation provides an opportunity to learn and grow, both individually and as partners, friends, or family members. Embracing mistakes as learning experiences can alleviate the pressure to communicate flawlessly. Instead of viewing communication as a performance, we can see it as an evolving practice that requires patience and compassion.

Building a supportive communication framework also involves seeking feedback. Encourage open dialogue about how you communicate with others. Ask for their perspectives on what works well and what could be improved. This feedback loop creates an atmosphere of growth, reinforcing the idea that communication is a shared journey rather than a solitary endeavor.

In conclusion, effective communication is the cornerstone of meaningful relationships. By practicing mindful listening, asking open-ended questions, expressing needs openly, and managing our emotions, we cultivate an environment where trust can flourish. We can navigate disagreements constructively and build a shared language that supports mutual understanding. With each conversation, we move closer to deeper connections with our loved ones, enriching our lives with the warmth of authentic relationships.

Ultimately, communication is not just a skill; it is an art form. It requires creativity, sensitivity, and a willingness to grow together. As we commit to this journey, we learn that each exchange is an opportunity to weave a richer tapestry of connection, trust, and intimacy in our relationships. Through mindful communication, we not only share our thoughts but also our hearts, forging bonds that withstand the test of time.

Chapter 4:

Cultivating Emotional Intimacy for Lasting Connection

Emotional intimacy is a cornerstone of meaningful relationships, yet it is often confused with physical closeness or shared experiences. While physical proximity can foster a sense of connection, emotional intimacy runs much deeper. It involves understanding, trust, and a shared vulnerability that allows individuals to feel safe in expressing their thoughts, feelings, and fears. This chapter will guide you through the journey of cultivating emotional intimacy with loved ones, emphasizing the importance of being present, empathetic, and genuinely invested in your relationships.

To begin, let's explore what it means to be **present** in our interactions. In our fast-paced world, where distractions are constant, being present can be a challenge. However, being fully engaged during conversations is essential to nurturing emotional intimacy. This means putting away your phone, making eye contact, and truly listening to what the other person is saying. When you give your full attention, you send a powerful message: "You matter to me."

Being present also involves understanding the unspoken feelings and emotions that may be at play during a conversation. For example, when a friend shares a story about a tough day, instead of jumping straight to offering solutions or advice, take a moment to acknowledge their feelings. You might say, "It sounds like you had a really hard day. I'm here for you." This simple statement not only validates their experience but also invites a deeper emotional connection.

Next, **empathy** is a crucial element in building emotional intimacy. Empathy goes beyond understanding someone's feelings; it involves feeling alongside them. It's about placing yourself in their shoes and genuinely trying to comprehend their experiences. When you approach your loved ones with empathy, you create a safe space for them to share their thoughts and emotions without fear of judgment.

To practice empathy, consider engaging in reflective listening exercises. When a loved one shares something significant, try to reflect back what you hear. For instance, if your partner expresses concern about a work issue, you might respond with, "I hear you're feeling stressed about your project at work and that it's weighing on your mind." This response shows that you are not only listening but also trying to understand their perspective, which fosters emotional closeness.

Being genuinely invested in a relationship means taking an active role in supporting the other person's emotional needs. This investment requires you to be attuned to their feelings, preferences, and aspirations. Consider the following exercise: set aside dedicated time to check in with your loved ones. Ask them how they are feeling, what challenges they are facing, and what joys they are experiencing. This practice encourages open dialogue and reinforces the idea that you care about their well-being.

As you work toward cultivating emotional intimacy, it's important to explore your own emotional layers and identify what you need to feel emotionally safe. Creating spaces for emotional safety is essential for both partners in any relationship. Emotional safety means feeling free to express your true self without fear of rejection or criticism. To foster this safety, consider sharing your own vulnerabilities with your loved ones. This might involve discussing your fears, insecurities, or past experiences. When you open up, you encourage others to do the same, creating a mutual exchange that strengthens your bond.

Throughout this chapter, guided exercises will help you deepen your emotional connections. One such exercise is the "Emotional Check-In." Set aside time with a loved one to discuss your emotions. Each person takes turns sharing how they have been feeling that week, without interruption. This exercise not only promotes active listening but also allows both individuals to understand each other's emotional landscapes better.

Another exercise is the "Appreciation Journal." Encourage each other to write down three things you appreciate about one another each week. At the end of the week, share these entries with each other. This practice reinforces positive feelings and helps you recognize the emotional value you bring to one another's lives.

As you explore the depths of emotional intimacy, you will inevitably encounter challenges. Relationships are not always smooth sailing; they require effort, understanding, and sometimes difficult conversations. Building resilience within your emotional connections is crucial. When conflicts arise, approach them with a mindset of curiosity rather than defensiveness. Ask open-ended questions to uncover the underlying emotions driving the conflict. For example, instead of saying, "You never listen to me," you might say, "I feel unheard when we discuss this issue. Can we talk about it?"

Celebrating joys together is equally important in strengthening emotional intimacy. Make it a habit to share good news and achievements, no matter how small. Celebrating each other's successes fosters a sense of partnership and joy that enriches the relationship. For instance, if your partner completes a challenging project at work, take the time to celebrate this milestone together, whether through a special dinner or a simple acknowledgment of their hard work.

Ultimately, cultivating emotional intimacy is a journey that requires patience, vulnerability, and a commitment to growth. As you implement the practices discussed in this chapter, you will notice a shift in your relationships. Emotional intimacy not only deepens your connections with loved ones but also enhances your ability to navigate challenges together.

The rewards of this journey are profound: a resilient bond that can withstand life's ups and downs, an emotional sanctuary where both individuals feel valued and understood, and a partnership that thrives on trust and authenticity. As you embrace the art of emotional intimacy, you'll find that your relationships transform into spaces of genuine connection, where love and understanding flourish.

As you continue on the path to cultivating emotional intimacy, it's essential to recognize that this process is ongoing. Relationships evolve over time, and so too must your understanding and practice of emotional intimacy. Here are some additional insights and strategies to enhance your journey.

Embracing Change

Change is a natural part of any relationship. Life events, personal growth, and shifting priorities can all impact how we connect with others. Embracing these changes rather than resisting them allows you to adapt and strengthen your emotional bonds. Engage in regular check-ins with your loved ones to discuss how each of you is feeling about the relationship. These conversations can reveal underlying feelings or concerns that may need to be addressed. For instance, if one partner feels overwhelmed with work and is withdrawing emotionally, having an open dialogue about it can create understanding and offer the support needed to navigate that phase together.

Practicing Forgiveness

Forgiveness is another crucial component of emotional intimacy. No one is perfect, and misunderstandings or hurt feelings can arise in any relationship. When conflicts occur, the ability to forgive is what allows the relationship to heal and grow stronger. It's vital to approach forgiveness not as a one-time act but as an ongoing practice. Start by acknowledging your feelings and the impact of the conflict. Then, express your willingness to move forward. For example, you might say, "I was hurt by what happened, but I value our relationship and want to work through this together."

Creating Rituals of Connection

Developing rituals of connection can also significantly enhance emotional intimacy. These rituals create opportunities for shared experiences and strengthen your bond. Consider establishing a weekly date night, a daily walk, or even a simple nightly routine of sharing three things you are grateful for that day. These moments of connection serve as anchors, reminding you of the importance of prioritizing each other amid life's busyness.

The Power of Vulnerability

As mentioned earlier, vulnerability is at the heart of emotional intimacy. It can be challenging to open up fully, but embracing vulnerability can lead to deeper understanding and connection. Consider discussing your dreams, fears, and aspirations with your loved ones. When you allow yourself to be seen in this way, you invite them to do the same. This mutual exchange of vulnerability fosters trust and creates an emotional landscape where both individuals feel safe and valued.

Building Emotional Resilience

Building emotional resilience is key to maintaining emotional intimacy, especially during challenging times. Resilience allows you to bounce back from difficulties and continue nurturing your connections. One way to build resilience is by developing problem-solving skills together. When faced with a challenge, approach it as a team. Instead of assigning blame, focus on finding solutions. For instance, if a disagreement arises over household responsibilities, brainstorm ways to share tasks that work for both partners. This collaborative approach not only resolves conflicts but also strengthens your partnership.

Recognizing and Addressing Emotional Triggers

Throughout your journey, you may encounter emotional triggers—specific situations or comments that evoke strong emotional responses. Recognizing these triggers is essential in fostering emotional intimacy. When you understand your triggers, you can communicate them to your loved ones, allowing them to support you better. For example, if you know that discussions about finances make you anxious, share this with your partner and suggest strategies to address these conversations more constructively.

Encouraging Growth Together

Emotional intimacy thrives in an environment where both individuals feel encouraged to grow and evolve. Support each other's personal development by setting shared goals. This could involve pursuing new hobbies, attending workshops, or exploring new interests together. As you engage in growth as a couple, you deepen your emotional connection, creating a shared sense of purpose that enhances intimacy.

Closing Thoughts

Cultivating emotional intimacy is a transformative journey that requires commitment, vulnerability, and a willingness to grow together. By being present, practicing empathy, and investing in your relationships, you create a strong foundation for emotional closeness. Remember that emotional intimacy is not merely about avoiding conflict but about facing challenges together, celebrating each other's successes, and fostering a space where both individuals feel safe to be themselves.

As you embrace these practices, you will not only enhance your emotional bonds but also enrich your life with deeper connections and lasting joy. The journey may have its challenges, but the rewards of emotional intimacy—trust, understanding, and a profound sense of connection—are invaluable treasures that make every effort worthwhile. With each step forward, you'll find that your relationships can withstand the test of time, creating a rich tapestry of shared experiences, joys, and memories that will sustain you both now and in the future.

Chapter 5:

Overcoming Barriers to Genuine Connection

In the journey of building meaningful relationships, even the most committed individuals encounter barriers that can impede genuine connection. These obstacles often stem from personal fears, past traumas, misunderstandings, or ingrained emotional responses. Recognizing and addressing these barriers is crucial for fostering deeper intimacy and authentic relationships. In this chapter, we will explore common obstacles that hinder connection and provide strategies for overcoming them, enabling you to create stronger, more resilient relationships.

Understanding Emotional Barriers

Emotional barriers can take many forms, but they typically manifest as walls that protect individuals from vulnerability. These barriers may be built from fear of rejection, past hurts, or a desire to maintain control over one's emotions. For example, someone who has been betrayed in a previous relationship may find it difficult to trust their current partner fully. They might consciously or subconsciously distance themselves, fearing that any display of vulnerability could lead to further pain.

Similarly, past trauma can lead to a heightened sensitivity to emotional triggers. A person who has experienced abandonment may struggle with the fear of losing their loved ones, prompting them to push others away to avoid potential heartache. These barriers, while protective in nature, ultimately hinder authentic connections.

Identifying Common Obstacles

To move past these barriers, it is essential to identify them. Common obstacles include:

1. **Fear of Rejection:** This fear often prevents individuals from expressing their true feelings or needs. The apprehension that one might be turned away or dismissed can create a significant barrier to intimacy.

2. **Past Trauma**: Previous experiences of betrayal, loss, or abandonment can leave lasting scars. These experiences can create a reluctance to trust or open up to new partners, leading to emotional distance.

3. **Misunderstandings**: Poor communication and assumptions can lead to misconceptions and conflicts. When individuals fail to articulate their thoughts or feelings clearly, it can result in hurt feelings and further emotional barriers.

4. **Perfectionism**: The desire to present oneself as perfect can stifle genuine connection. Individuals may fear being judged or criticized, leading them to conceal their true selves.

5. **Avoidance**: Some individuals may resort to avoidance as a coping mechanism. They may choose to withdraw rather than confront difficult emotions or conflicts, which only serves to deepen the divide in relationships.

Strategies for Overcoming Barriers

Overcoming these barriers requires intention, self-awareness, and effort. Here are some strategies to help you break down emotional walls and cultivate authentic connections:

1. Acknowledge and Confront Fears

The first step in overcoming fear is acknowledgment. Take time to reflect on what fears are holding you back from forming deeper connections. Journaling can be a powerful tool for this process. Write about your fears related to vulnerability, rejection, and intimacy. Once you've identified these fears, confront them by asking yourself whether they are based on current realities or rooted in past experiences.

For example, if you fear rejection, consider reflecting on your current relationship. Is there evidence that supports this fear? Often, fears are exaggerated by past experiences and may not hold true in your present context. Reframing these thoughts can help diminish their power over you.

2. Cultivate Trust Gradually

Trust is built over time and through shared experiences. Allow yourself to open up gradually with your loved ones. Start with small disclosures and observe how they respond. This process helps you gauge their reactions and establishes a foundation for deeper trust. Remember, vulnerability is not an all-or-nothing endeavor; it's a gradual unfolding of your inner self.

3. Practice Open Communication

Effective communication is essential for overcoming misunderstandings and fostering intimacy. Practice expressing your feelings and needs openly. Use "I" statements to communicate how you feel rather than placing blame. For example, instead of saying, "You never listen to me," try, "I feel unheard when I share my thoughts." This approach reduces defensiveness and encourages open dialogue.

Encourage your partner to share their feelings as well. Create a safe space for these discussions, free from interruptions or judgments. This mutual exchange fosters understanding and diminishes the likelihood of misunderstandings.

4. Work Through Past Hurts

Addressing past traumas can be challenging, but it is crucial for fostering emotional intimacy. Consider seeking professional support through therapy or counseling if past experiences significantly impact your ability to connect with others. A therapist can help you process your feelings, develop coping strategies, and gain insights into how your past affects your present relationships.

Additionally, engage in self-compassion practices. Acknowledge that healing takes time, and it is okay to feel vulnerable during this process. Embrace your emotions and allow yourself to feel the pain associated with past hurts without judgment. This self-acceptance can pave the way for healing and growth.

5. Recognize and Manage Triggers

Emotional triggers can derail conversations and lead to misunderstandings. Take time to reflect on what specific situations or comments trigger strong emotional responses. Once you identify these triggers, communicate them to your loved ones. For example, if discussions about future commitments make you anxious due to past experiences, share this concern with your partner.

When you feel a trigger arising, practice grounding techniques, such as deep breathing or taking a moment to step back from the conversation. This allows you to collect your thoughts and respond thoughtfully rather than reactively.

Building Resilience in Relationships

Creating stronger, more resilient relationships involves continuous effort. Embrace the mindset that relationships are a journey filled with ups and downs. Each obstacle you face together can serve as an opportunity for growth and deepening connection.

Engage in shared activities that promote teamwork and collaboration, such as problem-solving exercises or goal-setting discussions. By working together to overcome challenges, you foster a sense of partnership that strengthens your emotional bond.

Overcoming barriers to connection is a vital aspect of nurturing meaningful relationships. Acknowledging fears, addressing past traumas, practicing open communication, and recognizing triggers all contribute to breaking down emotional walls. As you implement these strategies, you empower yourself to create deeper, more authentic connections with those you love.

Remember that the journey toward emotional intimacy requires patience and perseverance. With each step you take, you move closer to fostering genuine relationships that can withstand life's challenges and celebrate its joys. Embrace the process, and allow yourself to connect on a deeper level, paving the way for lasting bonds filled with

trust, understanding, and love.

65

Chapter 6:

The Power of Shared Experiences

Shared experiences form the backbone of meaningful relationships. Whether it's a spontaneous weekend getaway, a regular family dinner, or a simple evening walk, these moments create a tapestry of memories that can strengthen bonds between individuals. In this chapter, we will explore the significance of spending quality time together, establishing shared goals, and honoring traditions. We will also discuss practical ways to incorporate connection-focused activities into your daily life, ensuring that the ties you form grow deeper over time.

The Importance of Quality Time

In today's fast-paced world, carving out quality time for loved ones can often feel like a daunting task. Yet, it is essential for nurturing intimacy and connection. Quality time isn't solely about the duration spent together; rather, it is about the depth of interaction and engagement during that time. When you are fully present with someone free from distractions and genuinely invested in the moment you create a safe space for connection to flourish.

Studies have shown that couples who prioritize spending quality time together report higher levels of satisfaction in their relationships. This time spent together can be transformative, as it allows for the sharing of thoughts, feelings, and experiences that might otherwise go unexpressed. Think of it as an investment in your relationship; the more effort you put into creating meaningful moments, the richer your connection becomes.

Creating Shared Goals

Shared goals can serve as a powerful catalyst for bonding. When two people work together toward a common objective, they strengthen their partnership and create a sense of unity. These goals can range from planning a family vacation to pursuing a joint fitness challenge or even embarking on a home improvement project. The key is to choose goals that resonate with both individuals and inspire collaboration.

For example, consider a couple looking to improve their health. By setting a goal to exercise together three times a week, they not only foster their physical well-being but also create shared experiences that promote intimacy. Each workout becomes an opportunity for encouragement, laughter, and growth—both as individuals and as a couple.

Establishing and Honoring Traditions

Traditions play a crucial role in fostering connection and continuity within relationships. They provide a framework for shared experiences that can be looked forward to and cherished over time. Establishing traditions doesn't have to be complex; they can be as simple as a weekly family movie night, a monthly date night, or an annual camping trip.

The beauty of traditions lies in their ability to create memories that anchor relationships. When you have rituals that bring you together, you develop a shared narrative that strengthens your bond. For instance, a family might gather every Sunday for a homemade brunch, where everyone contributes a dish. This not only promotes teamwork but also creates an opportunity for conversation and laughter, reinforcing family ties.

As you establish traditions, remember to honor them. Consistency is key; when you commit to these rituals, you show your loved ones that they are a priority in your life. This commitment fosters trust and security, making it easier for individuals to open up and be vulnerable with one another.

Making Time in a Busy World

Finding time for connection in today's busy world can be challenging. Work commitments, social obligations, and the myriad distractions of daily life can easily overshadow the importance of nurturing relationships. To combat this, intentionality is required. Here are some practical strategies for incorporating connection-focused activities into your life:

1. **Schedule Regular Check-Ins:** Just as you would schedule a meeting or appointment, block out time in your calendar for regular check-ins with loved ones. Whether it's a phone call, video chat, or in-person meeting, prioritize this time to connect and share what's happening in your lives.

2. **Create Daily Rituals**: Incorporate small daily rituals that promote connection. This could be enjoying morning coffee together, sharing a gratitude practice before bed, or taking a walk after dinner. These small moments can have a big impact on your relationship.

3. **Limit Distractions:** When you are spending time with loved ones, aim to minimize distractions. Put away phones and other devices to create a focused environment for connection. This practice reinforces the importance of being present with one another.

4. **Be Flexible and Creative:** Life can be unpredictable, so be open to adapting your plans. If a scheduled date night doesn't work out, consider a spontaneous picnic in the park or a movie night at home. The key is to find creative ways to connect, regardless of circumstances.

5. **Embrace Imperfection:** Remember that quality time doesn't always have to be perfect. It's about the intention behind the time spent together. Embrace the imperfections of life and find joy in the shared moments, even when things don't go as planned.

Connection-Focused Activities

Incorporating connection-focused activities into your life can create opportunities for shared experiences and deeper bonds. Here are a few ideas to inspire you:

1. **Cooking Together:** Prepare a meal as a team, experimenting with new recipes or making family favorites.

Cooking together encourages teamwork and allows for conversation and laughter.

2. **Volunteering:** Find a cause you both care about and volunteer together. This shared purpose not only strengthens your bond but also creates a sense of fulfillment and shared values.

3. **Exploring Nature**: Take walks, go hiking, or have picnics in nature. The tranquility of the outdoors can provide an ideal setting for meaningful conversations and shared experiences.

4. **Learning Together:** Choose a new hobby or skill to learn as a pair. Whether it's dancing, painting, or a new language, learning together fosters collaboration and can lead to shared accomplishments.

5. **Traveling:** Plan trips, whether near or far, to explore new places together. Travel creates shared memories that can be cherished for years to come.

The power of shared experiences cannot be overstated when it comes to nurturing relationships. By prioritizing quality time, establishing shared goals, and honoring traditions, you create a strong foundation for connection and intimacy. In a world that often prioritizes busyness over meaningful engagement, it is crucial to carve out space for your loved ones.

As you embark on this journey of cultivating shared experiences, remember that each moment spent together is an opportunity to deepen your bond. Embrace the joys and challenges that come with nurturing relationships, and celebrate the memories you create along the way. Through intentionality and commitment, you can forge connections that stand the test of time, enriching your life and the lives of those you cherish.

Chapter 7:

Navigating Trust and Intimacy in Romantic Relationships

Romantic relationships are unique in their complexity and depth. They often serve as the primary source of emotional support, love, and connection in our lives. However, with these profound rewards come specific challenges that can test the very fabric of our relationships. In this chapter, we will explore the dynamics of trust and intimacy in romantic connections, focusing on the delicate balance between independence and togetherness, the management of expectations, and the enhancement of emotional and physical intimacy. By addressing these aspects, we aim to provide couples with practical tools to cultivate a healthy and fulfilling partnership.

The Balance of Independence and Togetherness

One of the most critical dynamics in a romantic relationship is finding the right balance between independence and togetherness. It is essential for both partners to maintain their individuality while also nurturing their bond. Too much independence can lead to emotional distance, while too much togetherness can foster dependency and stifle personal growth.

To strike this balance, it's important to establish open communication about personal needs and desires. Each partner should feel comfortable expressing their interests, hobbies, and goals outside of the relationship. This independence can be empowering and beneficial, allowing each individual to grow and thrive both personally and as a couple.

At the same time, intentional time spent together is vital for deepening the emotional connection. Regular date nights, shared activities, and meaningful conversations help to reinforce the bond. These shared moments provide opportunities for growth, understanding, and intimacy, ultimately enriching the relationship.

Managing Expectations

Expectations can significantly impact the dynamics of a romantic relationship. Unmet expectations often lead to disappointment and frustration, which can erode trust over time. To manage expectations effectively, couples must communicate openly about their needs and desires.

Begin by discussing what each partner envisions for the relationship. What are your hopes for the future? What do you expect from each other in terms of support, affection, and commitment? This conversation can provide clarity and ensure that both partners are on the same page.

It's also important to recognize that relationships evolve over time. What you both need at the beginning of your journey together may change as you grow and face new challenges. Regularly checking in with each other about expectations allows for flexibility and adjustment, ensuring that both partners feel heard and valued.

Deepening Emotional and Physical Intimacy

Emotional and physical intimacy are intertwined and essential for a thriving romantic relationship. Emotional intimacy creates a safe space for vulnerability, allowing partners to share their thoughts, feelings, and fears without judgment. This openness fosters a deeper connection, as both individuals feel seen and understood.

To deepen emotional intimacy, engage in practices that promote vulnerability. This might involve sharing personal stories, discussing dreams, or exploring fears together. Activities like journaling about your feelings or practicing gratitude towards each other can also enhance emotional closeness.

Physical intimacy, while often perceived solely in sexual terms, encompasses a range of affectionate behaviors. Simple gestures, such as holding hands, cuddling, or sharing a long embrace, play a vital role in fostering connection. These acts of physical affection release oxytocin, the hormone associated with bonding, helping partners feel more secure and connected.

Constructive Conflict Resolution

Conflict is an inevitable aspect of any relationship, but how couples navigate these disagreements can significantly influence the health of their partnership. Constructive conflict resolution is crucial for maintaining trust and intimacy. Rather than avoiding conflicts or resorting to unhealthy communication patterns, couples should approach disagreements as opportunities for growth and understanding.

Begin by creating a safe environment for discussion. Choose an appropriate time and place to address conflicts, ensuring both partners feel calm and ready to communicate. Use "I" statements to express feelings without blaming the other person. For example, instead of saying, "You never listen to me," try, "I feel unheard when I share my thoughts." This approach fosters empathy and reduces defensiveness.

Active listening is another essential component of conflict resolution. Each partner should practice being fully present during discussions, listening to understand rather than to respond. Reflecting back what you hear can help clarify any misunderstandings and demonstrate that you value your partner's perspective.

If the conflict becomes heated, take a break and revisit the discussion later. This allows both partners to cool down and approach the situation with a clearer mindset. Ultimately, the goal is to find common ground and work toward a resolution that honors both partners' needs and feelings.

Prioritizing the Partnership

In the whirlwind of daily life, it's easy for couples to lose sight of the importance of prioritizing their partnership. Making a conscious effort to nurture the relationship can lead to greater satisfaction and connection. Couples should intentionally dedicate time to each other, whether through regular date nights, weekend getaways, or simple moments of connection at home.

Consider creating a relationship vision board together. Visualizing your shared goals, dreams, and aspirations can serve as a powerful reminder of your commitment to each other. This exercise allows both partners to express their desires for the future and fosters a sense of teamwork.

Exercises for Building Trust and Intimacy

To help couples cultivate a deeper connection, we offer the following exercises designed to promote open communication, vulnerability, and trust:

1. **The Trust-Building Conversation:** Set aside time to have a candid conversation about trust. Discuss what trust means to each of you, share past experiences that have influenced your views on trust, and identify any areas where you may need to rebuild trust.

2. **Vulnerability Sharing:** Each partner should take turns sharing a personal story or fear that they have not previously disclosed. This practice fosters vulnerability and encourages a deeper understanding of one another.

3. **Affection Inventory:** Take time to reflect on and list out the physical affection gestures that make you feel loved and appreciated. Share your lists with each other and commit to incorporating these gestures into your daily lives.

4. **Conflict Role Play:** Identify a recurring conflict in your relationship and role-play how you would like to handle it differently. Practice active listening and using "I" statements, allowing both partners to express their feelings.

6. **Gratitude Ritual:** At the end of each day, share three things you appreciate about each other. This practice promotes positivity and reinforces the emotional bond between partners.

Navigating trust and intimacy in romantic relationships requires intentionality, open communication, and a commitment to nurturing the partnership. By addressing the balance of independence and togetherness, managing expectations, deepening emotional and physical intimacy, and practicing constructive conflict resolution, couples can foster genuine connections rooted in respect and love.

As you embark on this journey together, remember that building trust and intimacy is an ongoing process. Embrace vulnerability, communicate openly, and prioritize your partnership. Through these practices, you can create a strong foundation for a lasting, fulfilling romantic relationship.

Chapter 8:

Strengthening Family Ties

Family relationships are among the most significant connections we forge throughout our lives. Yet, they can also be the most complicated. Each family has its own dynamics, shaped by individual personalities, experiences, and histories. Understanding these dynamics and cultivating trust and respect across generations is essential for nurturing a healthy family environment. This chapter will explore effective strategies to strengthen family ties, encourage open communication, and respect individual differences, enabling a culture of support and love within the family unit.

Understanding Family Dynamics

Every family operates within a unique set of dynamics influenced by relationships, roles, and expectations. Whether it's the nurturing parent, the rebellious child, or the wise grandparent, these roles can shift over time, and understanding how they affect interactions is crucial.

Begin by mapping out your family's structure and dynamics. Consider the relationships between family members: who is closest, who often disagrees, and who takes on leadership roles during family gatherings. Reflecting on these dynamics can illuminate patterns that might be creating tension or misunderstanding.

Once you have a clear picture, engage in open dialogues with family members about their feelings and perceptions. Encourage honesty and openness to create a safe space for expressing thoughts. Understanding each person's perspective will not only enhance empathy but also build a foundation for stronger connections.

Fostering Open Communication

Communication is the lifeblood of any relationship, and it is especially critical within families. Open communication helps to establish trust, resolve conflicts, and foster understanding. However, effective communication can be challenging in familial settings, where emotions run high, and past grievances often resurface.

To improve communication within your family, consider implementing the following strategies:

1. **Regular Family Meetings:** Establish a routine where family members can come together to discuss concerns, celebrate achievements, or simply share updates. This structured time allows everyone to feel heard and valued.

2. **Practice Active Listening:** Encourage family members to listen attentively without interrupting. Acknowledge each person's thoughts and feelings to demonstrate respect and understanding.

3. **Use "I" Statements**: When discussing sensitive topics, encourage family members to express their feelings using "I" statements. For example, "I feel overwhelmed when there's too much noise at home," rather than "You're

always making too much noise." This approach reduces defensiveness and encourages constructive conversations.

4. **Create Safe Spaces for Sharing:** Designate a specific time and place for family discussions that may be uncomfortable. Assure everyone that they can speak freely without fear of judgment or retaliation.

Respecting Differences

Families are often a tapestry of diverse personalities, beliefs, and values. Recognizing and respecting these differences is crucial for fostering a supportive family culture.

Start by acknowledging that every family member brings their unique perspective to the table. Instead of attempting to mold each person into a singular idea of "family," celebrate the diversity of thought and experience. This acknowledgment can lead to a richer family life, where everyone feels appreciated for who they are.

One effective method to respect differences is through family rituals that highlight individual strengths. For example, host themed nights where each family member can showcase something they love—cooking a favorite dish, sharing a hobby, or presenting a special talent. These moments can help family members appreciate each other's uniqueness while fostering bonds.

Supporting One Another Through Challenges

Life is filled with challenges, and families can either unite or divide during difficult times. How family members support one another can define the strength of their relationships.

Encouraging an atmosphere of support begins with cultivating emotional intelligence within the family. Teach family members to recognize their feelings and those of others. This empathy allows them to respond compassionately during tough times.

When a family member faces a challenge, whether it's academic struggles, health issues, or relationship difficulties, rally around them. Offer your presence, lend a listening ear, or provide practical help as needed. Creating a culture where asking for and offering help is normalized strengthens the familial bond.

Consider implementing a "family support network" where members can volunteer to assist one another during tough times. This could mean taking care of a sibling's children during a crisis, providing meals, or simply checking in regularly. Knowing they have a support system fosters resilience and deepens trust.

Building a Family Culture of Trust and Respect

To create a lasting family culture that values each member's unique qualities, it is crucial to cultivate trust and respect. Begin by modeling these values yourself. Show respect in your actions, decisions, and communication, demonstrating to others how to engage with one another.

One practical way to reinforce this culture is to establish family traditions that focus on trust and respect. For instance, creating a family motto or mission statement can guide behaviors and expectations. Include every family member in the process, allowing them to contribute ideas and express what trust and respect mean to them.

Additionally, celebrate achievements big and small within the family. Acknowledge milestones, whether academic, professional, or personal, and encourage family members to support each other's goals. This positive reinforcement fosters a sense of belonging and encourages members to invest in one another's success.

Strengthening family ties is an ongoing process that requires patience, understanding, and commitment. By understanding family dynamics, fostering open communication, respecting differences, and supporting one another through challenges, families can cultivate a nurturing environment. Embrace the uniqueness of each family member and create traditions that promote trust and respect.

Ultimately, the goal is to create a family culture where every individual feels valued, supported, and loved. As families learn to navigate complexities together, they forge deeper connections that will endure through life's trials and triumphs.

Chapter 9:

Nurturing Lifelong Friendships

Friendships are a cornerstone of human experience, providing us with joy, support, and companionship. However, the journey of friendship is rarely linear; it ebbs and flows through various life stages, influenced by circumstances, personal growth, and shifting priorities. This chapter delves into the unique aspects of friendship, offering practical guidance on how to cultivate and maintain these vital connections over time, even as they evolve.

The Importance of Friendships

Friendships contribute significantly to our overall well-being, serving as a source of comfort and understanding. Unlike familial or romantic relationships, friendships are often chosen, built on shared interests and experiences. This voluntary nature is what makes them particularly special, but it also means they require intentionality to nurture. Friendships can enrich our lives, providing laughter during tough times and a sense of belonging in a complex world.

Building Strong Foundations

To create and sustain deep friendships, it's essential to cultivate strong foundations based on active listening, shared values, and open communication.

1. **Active Listening**: One of the most critical aspects of any relationship is the ability to listen actively. This means giving your full attention to your friend, maintaining eye contact, and showing genuine interest in what they are saying. Reflect back on their feelings and thoughts to demonstrate your understanding. For instance, if a friend expresses frustration about work, instead of immediately offering advice, try saying, "That sounds really challenging. How do you feel about it?" This approach fosters trust and openness, making your friend feel valued and heard.

2. **Shared Values**: Identifying and nurturing shared values can deepen your friendship. Discuss what matters most to you both, whether it's family, career goals, or social causes. Shared values not only help in establishing a stronger connection but also provide a guiding framework for navigating challenges together. Engage in activities that reflect these values, such as volunteering for a cause you both care about or participating in discussions that inspire both of you.

3. **Open Communication**: Maintaining open lines of communication is vital. Encourage each other to share thoughts, feelings, and experiences honestly. Make it a habit to check in regularly, asking not only how your friend is doing but also how they feel about various aspects of their life. This ongoing dialogue builds a solid foundation of trust, allowing both of you to express vulnerabilities and seek support when needed.

Navigating Distance and Change

Friendships can be tested during periods of distance or significant life changes, such as moving to a new city, starting a family, or embarking on a new career. These transitions can be challenging, but they can also lead to new opportunities for connection.

1. **Stay Connected**: Distance does not have to mean disconnection. In today's digital age, technology allows us to maintain friendships from afar. Regular video calls, voice messages, or even old-fashioned letters can help bridge the gap. Consider scheduling a virtual movie night or a game session to keep the bond alive. Making an effort to connect shows that you value the friendship despite physical separation.

2. **Be Flexible**: As life circumstances change, be prepared to adapt the dynamics of your friendship. Understand that each person's availability may fluctuate based on their responsibilities and priorities. Embrace the fluidity of friendships by being open to new ways of connecting. If

traditional hangouts are no longer possible, suggest new activities that fit your current lifestyles.

3. **Celebrate Milestones**: Make it a point to celebrate important milestones in each other's lives, no matter the distance. Whether it's a birthday, promotion, or personal achievement, acknowledging these moments strengthens your connection. A simple text, a call, or a thoughtful gift can show your friend that you are present in their life, even from afar.

Handling Conflicts Gracefully

Conflicts are a natural part of any relationship, including friendships. How you handle disagreements can determine the longevity and strength of your connection.

1. **Address Issues Early:** When conflicts arise, it's essential to address them sooner rather than later. Delaying a conversation can lead to resentment and misunderstandings. Approach your friend calmly and

express your feelings using "I" statements. For example, "I felt hurt when I didn't hear from you during a tough time" focuses on your feelings rather than placing blame, fostering a more constructive conversation.

2. **Seek Understanding:** During conflicts, strive to understand your friend's perspective. Ask open-ended questions to encourage dialogue, such as "Can you help me understand what you were feeling?" This demonstrates that you value their feelings and are willing to work toward a resolution together. Practice active listening during these discussions to validate their experience.

3. **Find Common Ground**: Conflicts can often lead to growth if approached collaboratively. Identify shared goals and work together to find solutions that benefit both parties. This process not only resolves the current issue but can also strengthen your friendship as you learn to navigate challenges together.

Cultivating Mutual Support and Joy

As friendships mature, it's crucial to cultivate a culture of mutual support and joy. Celebrating each other's successes and providing comfort during difficult times enhances the bond you share.

1. **Share Life's Joys and Sorrows**: Make it a priority to be there for each other through life's ups and downs. Whether it's cheering on your friend during a significant event or offering a listening ear during tough times, your presence matters. These shared experiences build resilience and trust in your friendship.

2. **Create Lasting Memories:** Invest time in activities that create lasting memories. Plan outings, embark on adventures, or simply enjoy quiet evenings together. These shared experiences deepen your bond and provide a wealth of joyful moments to reflect on in the future.

3. **Express Appreciation**: Regularly express gratitude for your friend and the role they play in your life. Simple acknowledgments, whether verbal or through small gestures, can reinforce the connection you share. Let your friend know what you admire about them and how much you value their friendship.

Friendships are essential for our emotional well-being, but they require intentional effort to nurture and grow. By focusing on active listening, shared values, and open communication, you can build strong, lasting friendships. Embrace the changes that come with life and stay connected, even from a distance.

As you navigate conflicts, remember that handling them with grace and understanding can strengthen your bond. Ultimately, it's the mutual support, joy, and companionship that define true friendship. Commit to investing in these relationships, and you'll find that they enrich your life in countless ways.

Chapter 10:

Embracing a Life of Trust and Connection

As we conclude this journey through the intricate world of human relationships, it's essential to reflect on the vital elements that have shaped our understanding of trust, vulnerability, and emotional intimacy. Each of these aspects plays a critical role in fostering deeper connections with ourselves and others. This final chapter serves not only as a summary of the insights we've explored but as a powerful call to action: to integrate these lessons into the fabric of our daily lives and relationships.

The Foundation of Trust

Trust is the cornerstone of any meaningful relationship. It is built gradually through consistency, honesty, and reliability. To foster trust in your relationships, consider the following practices:

1. **Be Reliable**: Consistency in your actions and words is crucial. When you commit to something, whether it's a small favor or a major promise, follow through. Your reliability fosters an environment where others feel safe to rely on you.

2. **Communicate Openly**: Transparency is key to building trust. Share your thoughts and feelings openly, and encourage others to do the same. Create a space where questions are welcomed, and discussions can happen without fear of judgment.

3. **Address Breaches of Trust**: No relationship is immune to lapses in trust. When trust is broken, address it promptly. Have honest conversations about what went wrong, express your feelings, and work together to rebuild that trust through mutual effort.

The Strength in Vulnerability

Vulnerability is often seen as a weakness, but in truth, it is one of the most courageous things a person can do. It allows us to connect on a deeper level and to truly be seen by others. To embrace vulnerability in your relationships:

1. **Share Your Authentic Self**: Open up about your thoughts, fears, and dreams. Let others see you for who you truly are, imperfections and all. This authenticity encourages others to do the same, deepening your connection.

2. **Embrace Discomfort**: Understand that being vulnerable can feel uncomfortable. Acknowledge those feelings, and allow yourself to sit with them. Growth often comes from stepping outside your comfort zone, and vulnerability is a significant part of that process.

3. **Create a Safe Space for Others**: Foster an environment where others feel safe to express their vulnerabilities. Validate their feelings, listen without judgment, and show empathy. This mutual exchange creates a bond built on trust and respect.

Cultivating Emotional Intimacy

Emotional intimacy goes beyond mere physical closeness; it encompasses understanding, support, and deep connection. To enhance emotional intimacy in your relationships:

1. **Practice Active Listening**: Truly listen to what others are saying. Reflect back on their feelings and validate their experiences. This practice helps to create a deep sense of understanding and belonging.

2. **Engage in Meaningful Conversations**: Go beyond small talk. Ask open-ended questions that encourage others to share their thoughts and feelings. Share your own experiences, allowing for deeper discussions that strengthen your bond.

3. **Spend Quality Time Together**: Prioritize time with loved ones, engaging in activities that foster connection.

Whether it's a deep conversation over coffee or a shared hobby, these moments create lasting memories and deepen your relationship.

A Call to Action

Now that we have explored the foundations of trust, vulnerability, and emotional intimacy, it's time to take action. Here are practical steps to integrate these elements into your daily life and relationships:

1. **Set Intentions for Your Relationships:** Reflect on what you want from your relationships. Are there areas where trust needs to be rebuilt? Do you wish to be more vulnerable with certain individuals? Set clear intentions and commit to nurturing these aspects.

2. **Engage in Regular Check-Ins**: Establish routines for checking in with friends, family, and partners. Use these moments to share updates, express feelings, and discuss any concerns. These conversations help maintain open communication and strengthen bonds.

3. **Embrace New Connections**: Don't hesitate to reach out to new people. Pursue friendships and connections that resonate with you. Approach these interactions with an open heart, ready to share and embrace vulnerability.

4. **Reflect and Adapt**: Continuously reflect on your relationships. What's working well? What could be improved? Be willing to adapt and grow, both as an individual and within your relationships. This process of reflection fosters a deeper understanding of yourself and others.

The Journey Forward

Building a life centered on trust, vulnerability, and open communication is not a one-time effort but a lifelong journey. Each interaction, conversation, and shared experience contributes to the tapestry of your relationships. Embrace this journey wholeheartedly, knowing that it will lead to a supportive network of authentic connections that enhance personal growth and satisfaction.

As you move forward, remember that deepening your connections doesn't happen overnight. It requires patience, dedication, and a willingness to be vulnerable. The rewards of this investment are immeasurable: lasting bonds that withstand challenges, moments of joy shared, and a profound sense of belonging.

By embracing trust, vulnerability, and emotional intimacy in every aspect of your life, you pave the way for a richer, more fulfilling existence. Open your heart, take the leap, and step into a world where meaningful relationships thrive. Your journey toward deeper connection begins now, shaping a life filled with lasting, fulfilling bonds.

www.ingramcontent.com/pod-product-compliance
Lightning Source LLC
Chambersburg PA
CBHW061359250726
48657CB00004B/1573